CONTENTS

INTRODUCTION

In today's competitive job market, securing your dream job consists of more than just a stellar resume and impressive credentials. It demands preparation, confidence, and a deep understanding of the interview process. Whether you're a seasoned professional seeking career advancement or a recent graduate stepping into the workforce for the first time, mastering the art of the interview is essential for success.

Welcome to "Mastering the Interview: Top 39 Interview Questions and How to Interpret What the Question is Really Asking, Written By A Current Hiring Manager." In this comprehensive guide, I delve into the most common and challenging questions asked during job interviews and decode their true meaning.

Interviews can be daunting experiences, filled with uncertainty and pressure. But they also present incredible opportunities to showcase your skills, experiences, and unique qualities to potential employers. By understanding the types of questions you're likely to encounter and preparing thoughtful, well-articulated responses, you can approach any interview with confidence and poise.

Throughout this book, I'll explore a wide range of topics, from your professional background and qualifications to your strengths,

MASTERING THE INTERVIEW

Top 39 Interview Questions and
How to Interpret What the Question
is Really Asking, Written By A
Current Hiring Manager

By

Scott B.

weaknesses, and motivations. I'll provide detailed interpretations of each question, along with valuable insights and tips to help you craft your own responses effectively. Focus on the interpretation of the questions to help eliminate the anxiety and stress of the interview process.

Whether you're facing your first job interview or looking to refine your interview skills, "Mastering the Interview" is your ultimate companion on the journey to career success. By studying and internalizing the strategies and techniques outlined in this book, you'll be well-equipped to navigate any interview scenario and leave a lasting impression on hiring managers.

A quick note about the author of this book – I have been a Hiring Manager for many different companies in sales, marketing, healthcare, restaurant, and pool/spa industry, to name a few. I felt compelled to put this information together to educate, prepare, and eliminate the unnecessary stress of the interview itself. I have personally interviewed countless potential job candidates who very well may have been a great fit for the position but came to the interview grossly unprepared. I have reviewed several other information books, blogs, and podcasts on this topic. While some of them are very good, others are written by interview advisors, not the Manager tasked with making the final decision. This book will give you direct information from an actual Hiring Manager who is still in this current role. For each question listed, you will see the "standard guidance" in regular print, then the interpretation in italics.

One last note before we get into the questions: all job candidates are unique and come from all walks of life. It does not matter where you are in your career. You could be just starting out, a recent college graduate, someone looking to change careers, or an older adult getting back into the workforce. These questions and suggested responses will still apply, but you must "tweak" the answers to fit your unique situation.

So, are you ready to unlock the secrets to facing your next interview? Let's dive in and discover how you can confidently tackle the top 39 interview questions and land the job of your dreams.

1. Tell me about yourself.

- Answer: Start with a short overview of your professional background, focusing on relevant experiences and skills. Mention your career goals and how this position aligns with them.

- This is by far the most common opening question. This question is generally aimed at making sure the potential candidate can carry on a conversation and for the manager to get an initial feel for your personality.

🖹 Notes:

_____

_____

_____

_____

_____

_____

_____

_____

_____

_____

_____

_____

2. Why do you want to work for this company?

- Answer: Research the company and mention specific aspects like its culture, mission, or reputation that appeal to you. Explain how you believe you can contribute to its success.

- *Another point to mention here if it applies to your situation, if you know someone who currently works for the company and enjoys their job, this is a good time to bring that up. If not, there is obviously some reason why you applied, just be sure to keep it professional.*

🗒 Notes:

_____

_____

_____

_____

_____

_____

_____

_____

_____

_____

3. Why are you interested in this position?

- Answer: Highlight aspects of the job description that excite you and align with your skills and interests.

- *Discuss the job posting specifically and what triggered you to apply. The manager wants to see some effort on your part here and to show you've done at least a little bit of homework.*

📋 Notes:

_____

_____

_____

_____

_____

_____

_____

_____

_____

_____

_____

_____

4. What are your strengths?

- Answer: Choose strengths relevant to the job and provide examples of how you've demonstrated them in previous roles.

- *Alot of candidates here generally give some standard responses that include: hard working, attention to detail, dependable, etc. If you plan to use attention to detail, be prepared to give an example of this. I have interviewed potential candidates who give this as a strength, and there are typos in their resumes. Some good alternative discussion points to use here would be: creative, solution driven, customer focused, presentations, etc., and be sure to have examples to expand on these.*

🗒 Notes:

_____

_____

_____

_____

_____

_____

_____

_____

_____

_____

_____

5. What are your weaknesses?

- Answer: Discuss a weakness you've identified and how you're actively working to improve it. Emphasize your willingness to learn and grow.

- *This is a topic most everyone is hesitant to answer. Keep in mind, the main goal for this question is to give an example of something you have identified in the past that you were not comfortable with and what steps you took to overcome it. Remember, no one is perfect!.*

🗐 Notes:

_____

_____

_____

_____

_____

_____

_____

_____

_____

_____

_____

_____

6. Where do you see yourself in five years?

- Answer: Discuss your long-term career goals and how you envision progressing within the company. Emphasize your commitment to growth and development.

- *This question is generally asked by the Hiring Manager to get a "feel" to see if you are looking at this position as a long-term decision to grow or just a stepping stone to beef up your resume.*

🗒 Notes:

_____

_____

_____

_____

_____

_____

_____

_____

_____

_____

_____

7. Why should we hire you?

- Answer: Summarize your qualifications and experiences that make you the best fit for the role.

- *As the candidate, you may not know all the specifics of the job, the company culture, etc., but what the question is really asking is why should the company dedicate time and financial resources to invest in your training? A good response here would re-visit your five year plan response and communicate your commitment to the company as a whole, with a focus on growing both professionally and personally in your role.*

🖺 Notes:

_____

_____

_____

_____

_____

_____

_____

_____

_____

_____

8. What motivates you?

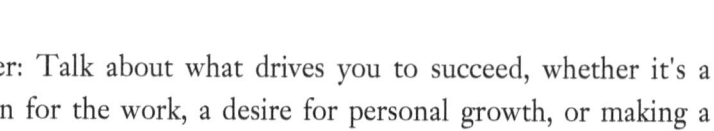

- Answer: Talk about what drives you to succeed, whether it's a passion for the work, a desire for personal growth, or making a positive impact. Provide examples of times when you felt particularly motivated.

- *This one is pretty straightforward; the Manager is trying to decipher if you are just in it for the money or if this role will help support your motivations.*

🗒 Notes:

_____

_____

_____

_____

_____

_____

_____

_____

_____

_____

_____

_____

9. Can you provide an example of a time when you demonstrated leadership skills?

- Answer: Describe a situation where you led a team or took initiative to solve a problem. Highlight your ability to inspire others, make decisions, and achieve goals.

- *If interviewing for a leadership position, this answer is crucial. Describe your leadership style, discuss building a team, and give examples of how you involve team members in decision making. If it's not a leadership position, the manager may be trying to get a sense of your openness for leadership.*

🖹 Notes:

_____

_____

_____

_____

_____

_____

_____

_____

_____

10. How do you handle stress and pressure?

———— ∞ ————

- Answer: Discuss specific strategies you use to manage stress effectively, such as prioritizing tasks, staying organized, or practicing mindfulness.

- *Every job has it's stressors, which are different for everyone. This is not a trick question or asked to disqualify you. Some good answers here are exercising, journaling, going for a walk to disconnect, etc.*

🗒 Notes:

_____

_____

_____

_____

_____

_____

_____

_____

_____

_____

_____

_____

11. Describe a time when you had to work as part of a team.

- Answer: Choose an example that demonstrates your ability to collaborate with others towards a common goal. Discuss your role on the team and how you contributed to its success.

- *This is a common question that the Manager is trying to determine if you would be a good team member. If you have an example to give then great. If this is your first job, give an example of a team environment outside of work.*

🗐 Notes:

_____

_____

_____

_____

_____

_____

_____

_____

_____

_____

_____

12. What do you know about our products/services?

- Answer: Demonstrate your knowledge of the company's offerings and how they address customer needs.

- *This is where you will need to do a bit of homework to learn what the company does and how it affects its customers. It's always a good idea to do some research on the company you are applying for.*

📋 Notes:

_____

_____

_____

_____

_____

_____

_____

_____

_____

_____

_____

13. Can you give an example of a time when you had to resolve a conflict with a coworker?

- Answer: Describe a conflict you encountered and how you approached resolving it professionally. Emphasize your communication and conflict resolution skills.

- *From time to time, all coworkers will have a conflict of some sort. It's not unacceptable for this to happen. What the Manager is looking for is what steps you took to resolve it, how do you communicate your differences, and what was the ultimate resolution.*

🖹 Notes:

_____

_____

_____

_____

_____

_____

_____

_____

14. How do you stay organized, focused, and prioritize tasks?

———— ⌘ ————

- Answer: Discuss your methods for managing your workload efficiently, such as using to-do lists or project management tools. Highlight your ability to prioritize tasks based on importance and deadlines.

- *In most all jobs, you will get tasks assigned to you even though you are working on current responsibilities. The Manager is trying to get a feel for how you keep track of your tasks and how you determine priority.*

🖺 Notes:

_____

_____

_____

_____

_____

_____

_____

_____

_____

_____

_____

15. Discuss a time when you had to meet a tight deadline.

- Answer: Talk about a time when you had to work efficiently to complete a project on time. Describe the actions you took to prioritize tasks and deliver results under pressure.

- *This is similar to the previous question, just asked differently. This is just a bit more focused on prioritization. Be sure to mention that you have reached out to your previous manager to determine prioritization. Hiring managers like to hear that the candidate looked to the manager to help determine priorities.*

📋 Notes:

_____

_____

_____

_____

_____

_____

_____

_____

_____

_____

16. How do you handle constructive criticism?

- Answer: Emphasize your openness to feedback and willingness to learn and improve.

- *Another reminder here that no one is perfect. Be sure to mention that. Constructive criticism is a common practice in the workplace and communicating that you are not offended by this practice is crucial. Feedback is essential for growth!*

🗒 Notes:

_____

_____

_____

_____

_____

_____

_____

_____

_____

_____

_____

17. Can you describe a time when you had to learn a new skill or technology quickly?

- Answer: Talk about a situation where you had to adapt to new tools or processes to perform your job effectively. Describe the steps you took to learn and master the skill or technology.

- *Constant learning is essential for any job. New ideas and new tools to help improve efficiency and job tasks will always be a workplace practice. Communicating that you are open to new ideas to help improve efficiency is a strong response to this one. Give a personal example if you have one.*

🗒 Notes:

_____

_____

_____

_____

_____

_____

_____

_____

_____

18. What do you think sets you apart from other candidates?

- Answer: Highlight your unique qualities, skills, and experiences that make you the best fit for the role. Provide specific examples that demonstrate your strengths.

- *If you have specific past experience that is applicable to the position you are applying for, this is a good time to discuss it. If not, lean more toward you as an individual, your ability to work well with others, proven ability to prioritize, friendly disposition, etc.*

🖹 Notes:

_____

_____

_____

_____

_____

_____

_____

_____

_____

_____

_____

19. Can you describe a time when you had to persuade others to see your point of view?

- Answer: Describe a situation where you successfully influenced others to adopt your perspective or support your ideas. Discuss the strategies you used to communicate effectively and gain buy-in.

- *This question is aimed at presenting the manager with an example of utilizing teamwork, how you collaborate, and discussing your ideas when compared to other suggested options. Even if your idea wasn't implemented you can still speak to that example of what steps you took to make sure your option was considered.*

🗒 Notes:

_____

_____

_____

_____

_____

_____

_____

_____

_____

20. Describe a time when you had to take initiative and lead a project.

- Answer: Talk about a project or initiative you spearheaded, from conception to completion. Describe the steps you took to plan, organize, and execute the project, as well as the results you achieved.

- *This is just another example of talking about your experiences with working with a team. If you have a project in the past where you were delegated the lead role and how you organized your team, then great! However, it's okay to use a non-work example for this as well. (ex. Church, school, or sports team project) The goal here is to provide an example of your approach to planning and team organization.*

🗒 Notes:

_____

_____

_____

_____

_____

_____

21. How do you handle feedback from your manager or colleagues?

- Answer: Discuss your approach to receiving feedback with an open mind and a focus on improvement.

- *This could be another way to ask about constructive criticism. Accepting feedback is something you will experience on the job or when taking part in outside projects. Focus on your response to demonstrate the ability to accept feedback to allow for personal growth and improvement.*

🗐 Notes:

_____

_____

_____

_____

_____

_____

_____

_____

_____

22. Can you describe a time when you had to work with a difficult coworker or client?

- Answer: Talk about a challenging interpersonal situation you encountered and how you handled it professionally. Discuss the strategies you used to communicate effectively and resolve conflicts.

- *Addressing a client example, one thing to emphasize is your ability to listen and try to understand why the client is upset or is coming across as difficult. Discuss the importance of empathy and a mutual understanding to determine a solution. The manager is trying to determine how you would respond to an upset client. Coworkers present a unique challenge as they will be involved with you more often. Again, stressing your ability to listen and your ability to reach a mutual resolution is the main goal to express.*

🗒 Notes:

_____

_____

_____

_____

_____

_____

23. How do you stay motivated in your work?

- Answer: Discuss what motivates you to excel in your job, whether it's a passion for the work, a desire for personal growth, or external factors like recognition or advancement. Provide examples of times when you felt particularly motivated.

- *Motivation is different for everyone. For some it will be just about the money. For others, they find motivation in personal or team recognition. There is really no incorrect response on this, but try to communicate more of a team recognition approach as opposed to a "me" approach.*

🗒 Notes:

_____

_____

_____

_____

_____

_____

_____

_____

_____

_____

24. Can you provide an example of a time when you had to adapt to a change in the workplace?

- Answer: Describe a situation where you faced a significant change and how you successfully adapted to it. Discuss the strategies you used to embrace change positively.

- *The goal of this question is for the manager to determine how you would potentially respond to change in the workplace. If you have an example to share from a previous job, this is a great time to bring that up. It could be something as simple as a previous manager or supervisor asking you to add some additional detail to a report or changing the way you perform your task. Expressing the ability to be positive and open to change is the goal for the answer.*

🗒 Notes:

_____

_____

_____

_____

_____

_____

_____

25. Do you prefer working independently or as part of a team, or both?

- Answer: Talk about your ability to excel in both independent and team settings. Discuss situations where you've demonstrated success in each scenario.

- *There is constant opportunity in the workplace to be a part of a team and work on your own. The goal for the answer here is to express your understanding of the importance of each approach and why you would excel in both scenarios. Tip – if you emphasize one over the other too much, it could disqualify you in the manager's eyes, depending on the position you are interviewing for.*

🗒 Notes:

_____

_____

_____

_____

_____

_____

_____

26. What are your salary expectations?

- Answer: Research industry standards and the company's salary range for the position. Provide a range based on your research and your own experience and qualifications.

- *This is one of the hardest questions to answer, as you don't want to say a number too high or too low. Yes, do some research before your interview in case you are asked this and it is perfectly okay to ask what the salary range is for this position. One point I must emphasize- if the interviewer does not bring up salary or money, you should not either. Depending on the specific company structure ,they may not be the decision-maker on the salary offer.*

🗐 Notes:

_____

_____

_____

_____

_____

_____

_____

_____

27. Can you discuss a time when you had to learn from a mistake?

- Answer: Talk about a specific mistake you made, what you learned from it, and how you applied that knowledge to future situations. Emphasize your ability to take responsibility and grow from failures.

- *Once again, no one is perfect and we all make mistakes. It's perfectly okay to vocalize this, but for the mistake you will speak to, be sure you have a follow-up example of how you learned from it and what you changed from that learning to minimize the chance of that same mistake happening again.*

🗒 Notes:

_____

_____

_____

_____

_____

_____

_____

28. What relevant experience do you have for this position?

- Answer: Highlight specific experiences and skills that directly relate to the job requirements. Provide examples that demonstrate your qualifications for the role.

- *This is an opportunity to speak directly to the job description and what you may have done in the past, that directly relates. Tip – when coming to your interview, bring a copy of the job posting with you. Highlight the specific areas you want to speak about, as during the interview process, you may forget what you wanted to discuss.*

🗒 Notes:

_____

_____

_____

_____

_____

_____

_____

_____

_____

_____

29. How do you make sure that you stay updated with industry trends and developments?

- Answer: Talk about the resources you use to stay informed, such as industry publications, professional networks, or continuing education opportunities.

- *Several positions, especially technical in nature, require ongoing learning and keeping up to date with the most recent approaches. If this applies to the position you are interviewing for, express why you feel it is important to stay up to date with current information. It is completely okay to ask how the company supports this crucial process.*

Notes:

_____

_____

_____

_____

_____

_____

_____

_____

30. Can you provide an example of a time when you had to deal with ambiguity or uncertainty?

- Answer: Describe a situation where you had to navigate uncertainty and make decisions with incomplete information. Discuss the strategies you used to gather relevant information and make informed choices.

- *Not all decisions are made with all the proper information as possible. Sometimes deadlines and restraints force you to decide before gathering all possible information. The goal here is to express that you would make every attempt to gather all the necessary information to make the best decision possible. Good to add to your response here that when faced with this specific scenario, you would consult your manager for input.*

🗐 Notes:

_____

_____

_____

_____

_____

_____

_____

31. What do you consider your greatest professional achievement?

- Answer: Talk about a significant accomplishment that demonstrates your skills, leadership abilities, or contributions to a team or organization. Highlight the impact of your achievement and what you learned from the experience.

- *If this is your first job, you may not have work experience to speak to. You could possibly use a college graduation as your greatest achievement to date. If you are a seasoned worker and have past experiences, emphasize a project or example where something you completed had a large impact on the company, operation efficiency, or process improvement.*

🗒 Notes:

_____

_____

_____

_____

_____

_____

_____

_____

32. How do you handle working with people who have different work styles or personalities?

- Answer: Discuss your ability to adapt to different work styles and personalities and collaborate effectively with diverse teams. Emphasize your communication and interpersonal skills.

- *This question directly tries to give the manager an example of how you communicate. It's also very important here to express in your response that different styles, different ideas and different approaches are a necessity for effective collaboration and overall best decision making.*

🖹 Notes:

_____

_____

_____

_____

_____

_____

_____

_____

_____

33. Can you discuss a time when you had to make a difficult decision at work?

- Answer: Describe a challenging decision you had to make, the influences you considered, and the outcome of your decision.

- *The focus of this question is to see how you explore options in your decision making and applied reason to making the decision. It's not so much about what the decision was, as opposed to how you came to the decision you made.*

🗎 Notes:

_____

_____

_____

_____

_____

_____

_____

_____

_____

34. What do you do if you disagree with your manager's decision?

- Answer: Discuss your approach to handling disagreements professionally and respectfully. Emphasize your willingness to voice concerns constructively and work towards finding a resolution.

- *First and foremost, know that it is okay to disagree with your manager's decision or the decision he / she is about to make. Here is another opportunity to discuss how you collaborate and communicate your ideas in a professional way. If you find yourself getting a lot of questions around this, this is a clear sign that you and your manager will be collaborating on many decisions and the manager is trying to get a feel of how these discussions would go.*

🗐 Notes:

_____

_____

_____

_____

_____

_____

35. How do you prioritize your professional development and learning?

- Answer: Talk about your commitment to ongoing learning and professional growth. Discuss the steps you take to identify areas for improvement and pursue relevant training or development opportunities.

- *This one is similar to a previous question, but asked in a little different way. Discuss how important and vital it is to stay up to date on current information regarding your position and how it fits into the overall company vision and growth. Once again, it is perfectly acceptable to ask how the company supports this commitment. Generally speaking, if the company finds this topic to be important, it should be understood that continuous learning will very likely be required.*

🗒 Notes:

_____

_____

_____

_____

_____

_____

36. What do you do if you're struggling to meet a deadline?

- Answer: Discuss your approach to managing deadlines and handling challenges. Talk about the steps you take to assess the situation, communicate proactively, and seek assistance if needed.

- *In this question, the manager is trying to get a feel to see if you think and operate in the moment or if you exercise to think one to two steps ahead and what that might look like. Deadlines are challenging in any industry and communicating that you would not hesitate that you need some guidance and assistance is a great answer here. Never be afraid to ask for assistance, you don't know what you don't know, it's a simple as that!*

🗒 Notes:

_____

_____

_____

_____

_____

_____

_____

_____

_____

37. Can you discuss a time when you had to work with limited resources?

- Answer: Describe an example where you had to complete a task or project with limited resources, such as time, budget, or manpower. Discuss the strategies you used to maximize efficiency and achieve your goals.

- *This question is a bit tricky in that the manager is trying to see how you would respond to limited resources and this could be time or money. If limited resources are an issue, you will know that very soon into the project. This is where the anticipation of tasks and planning comes into play. Describe ways you looked to consolidate tasks or utilize people on your team in the most efficient way.*

🗒 Notes:

_____

_____

_____

_____

_____

_____

_____

38. What do you do if you encounter resistance when implementing a new idea or initiative?

- Answer: Describe your approach to gaining buy-in and overcoming resistance to change. Discuss the strategies you use to communicate the benefits of your idea and address concerns effectively.

- *This will happen, you can bet on it! Discussing the importance of a positive attitude and acknowledging the team's resistance is key here. Your role is to likely implement a new idea, process, or whatever. You have to take the approach of "owning" that positive attitude. Resistance to anything new is human nature, be sure to express this in your response and discuss ways to eventually overcome the resistance.*

🗒 Notes:

_____

_____

_____

_____

_____

_____

39. How do you stay productive when working remotely?

- Answer: Discuss your strategies for staying focused and motivated while working remotely, such as setting a dedicated workspace, maintaining a routine, and staying connected with colleagues.

- *If you have never worked remote, your responses here should be around discussing this topic with someone you know who worked remote. For example, my good friend John works remote and he feels the most common distractions are... (fill in the blank here with things you think would be a distraction)*

🗒 Notes:

_____

_____

_____

_____

_____

_____

_____

_____

_____

_____

SOME ADDITIONAL TIPS

Remember to adjust your responses to the specific job and company you're interviewing for, and practice your answers beforehand to ensure you're prepared for the interview.

In almost all cases, you will get the "Do you have any questions for me?" question. You should never respond with a no. Even if you don't have a question, the below questions are perfectly acceptable to ask the manager in any interview:

What are the favorite parts of your job?

How long have you been with the company?

What was your position when you started?

Does the company have a history of promoting within?

Why did you decide to apply to work for this company?

How did this position become available?

I cannot emphasize enough to make sure you ask two to three questions. Re-read that statement again to make sure you understand the importance of this. If necessary, write these questions down and take them with you to the interview.

CONCLUSION

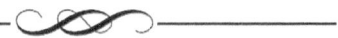

Congratulations! You've reached the end of "Mastering the Interview: Top 39 Interview Questions and How to Interpret What the Question is Really Asking, Written By A Current Hiring Manager." I hope that this book has provided you with valuable insights, strategies, and confidence to tackle even the toughest job interviews with ease.

Throughout these pages, we've explored the most common and challenging questions that candidates face during interviews, ranging from inquiries about your professional background and qualifications to your strengths, weaknesses, and aspirations. I've provided interpretations to each question, along with tips and real-world examples to help you craft compelling responses that showcase your skills and experiences effectively.

But remember, mastering the interview is not just about memorizing answers—it's about understanding yourself, your goals, and how you can add value to a potential employer. It's about building rapport, demonstrating your expertise, and showcasing your unique qualities and strengths.

As you prepare for your next interview, I encourage you to continue practicing and refining your responses, tailoring them to each specific job opportunity and company culture. Take advantage of mock interviews, networking opportunities, and feedback from mentors or trusted colleagues to hone your interview skills further.

And always remember the importance of confidence, positivity, and authenticity. Be yourself, stay calm under pressure, and approach each interview as an opportunity to shine and make a lasting impression.

I wish you the best of luck on your journey to career success. May you walk into every interview room with confidence, poise, and the knowledge that you are well-prepared to tackle any question that comes your way.

Finally - Always remember that an interview is basically a glorified conversation that is structured so that both you and the interviewer can learn things about each other and the company.

MASTERING THE INTERVIEW

Now that you have a better understanding of the top interview questions and their decoded meaning, it's time to pass on your newfound knowledge to show other readers where they can find the same help.

I am truly on a mission to help people get the job they desire with providing real interpretations of complex interview questions. I enjoy seeing the expressions on the individual's faces and feeling their positive body language when they are offered the job.

By simply leaving your honest opinion of this book on Amazon, you'll show other people preparing for their interviews where they can find information that will help them better prepare for their own interviews.

Thank you for your help. Mastering the Interview is kept alive when we take a moment to pass on our knowledge – and you are helping me do just that. Your review just might be the one that helps another successfully get that job.

Thank you for choosing "Mastering the Interview" as your guide. Here's to your future success!

Warm regards,

Please Leave a Review